# Verses of the Heart

Crescent Books

# Praise for *Verses of the Heart*

"These verses truly touch the reader's heart ...
beautiful collection, indeed."

**—Dr. Naser Bresa, author of** *Retrospektiva*

"Another set of beautiful poems by Flamur.
They are so captivating that I had to read them all at once.
Truly heart touching!"

**—Dr. Amber Haque, co-editor of** *Islamic Psychology Around the Globe*

"Flamur is adept at blending matters of the heart with
earthly matters. He is adept at highlighting
many of the world's perpetual afflictions. Some simply
do not see, or worse, see and do not care.
But if you find you are among those who are prepared
to make a change and are ready to let the
healing begin, I would first prescribe reading
*Verses of the Heart.*"

**—Brandon Mayfield, author of** *Grains of Destiny*

"If we are to heal ourselves, our communities, our nations and our world, we must find ways to speak to the heart. Flamur offers through his poetry that speaks to the heart the opportunity to heal ourselves and the world."

**—Dr. Miles Davis, president of Linfield University**

"Flamur continues to remind us to look with awe for the hidden beauty all around us. He seems to see light in the most grim of circumstances reminding us of Rumi's saying, 'There are beautiful things you can only see in the dark.'"

**—Dr. Omar Reda, author of**
***On the Shoulders of the Prophet***

"Every time I read Flamur Vehapi's poetry, I marvel at his illuminating wisdom. *Verses of the Heart* is a welcome beacon of light during these dark times. His inspirational words remind us that change must begin within our own hearts."

**—Paul Fattig, author of *Madstone***

"Flamur's verses present a spirit of optimism at a time when people are increasingly, physically and spiritually, moving away from one other. While highlighting the challenges of our times, he also gives us the recipe for solving the problem: our sense of humanity as a unifying element."

**—Dr. Eduart Caka, author of *Dialogu Ndërfetar*
and translator of *Devlet-i Aliyye***

**Also by Flamur Vehapi**

*The Adhan: A Brief Chronology,* 2026
*The Book of Great Quotes,* 2025 (2nd ed.)
*Berke Khan of the Golden Horde,* 2024
*The World According to Sami Frashëri,* 2024
*Kosovo: A Brief Chronology,* 2023
*Verses of the Heart: Poems,* 2021
*Ertugrul Ghazi: A Very Short Biography,* 2021
*The Book of Albanian Sayings: Cultural Proverbs,* 2017
*Peace and Conflict Resolution in Islam,* 2016
*A Cup with Rumi: Poems,* 2015
*The Alchemy of Mind: Poems,* 2016 (2nd ed.)
*Sfidat Jetike: Poezi,* 2002

**Translations**
*The Expansion of Islam by Sami Frashëri,* 2025 (2nd ed.)
*The Album of Aphorisms by Sami Frashëri,* 2019

# Verses of the Heart

New and Selected Poems

Flamur Vehapi
Introduction by David Jalajel

Crescent Books

Copyright © 2021 by Flamur Vehapi
First Published in December 2021
by Crescent Books
an imprint of Crescent Institute LLC
Portland, OR.
All rights reserved. No part of this publication
may be reproduced,
stored in any retrieval system, or transmitted, in any form
or by any means, electronic, mechanical, photocopying, recording or
otherwise without prior written
permission from the publisher.

Prepared and Typeset
by Elipse Productions

ISBN: 978-1-954935-01-3
1. Poems 2. Quotes 3. Poets
4. Biographies

First edition
Includes biographical references and appendices
Cover design by Erzen Pashaj
Cover art by Elipse Productions

Printed in the United States of America

To my beloved parents, as well as to
Suhail and Ryanne.
To my brother, sister, and their families,
as well as other relatives and friends
who have inspired me and served
as the cornerstone of my work.

And to all who have become
refugees at some point in their life.

## Acknowledgments

I am grateful to so many inspiring individuals who have assisted me with this collection, and to everyone who took the time to read this humble work and share their invaluable feedback with me. Also, thank you to the following for your support and mentorship: Salma and Masud Ahmad, Joel Hayward, Omar Reda, Amber Haque, Burhan Fili, Didmar Faja, Erzen Pashaj, Brandon Mayfield, David Jalajel, Naser Bresa, Paul Fattig, Maqsood Chaudhary, BJ Seda, Mehmet Yavuz, Dana Lundell, Miles Davis, Marisa Petersen, Stella Williams, Arber Gashi, Lavdrim Lipovica, Dren Qerimi, and to many more even if I did not mention you here. Their input and/or support has greatly enriched the book at hand as well as my previous ones. And special thanks to the following for their kind permission to use some of the quoted materials in this collection: Joel Hayward, Charles Upton, Mustansir Mir, Jennifer Boutz, Yahiya Emerick, and the NYU Press staff.

*"You and I
have to live
As if you and I
have never heard
of a you
and
an I."*[4]

— Jalal al-Din Muhammad Rumi

# Contents

| | |
|---|---|
| Acknowledgments | 11 |
| Preface | 17 |
| A note from the author | 21 |
| Introduction | 25 |
| | |
| Our humanity | 27 |
| Enough | 29 |
| COVID-19 | 31 |
| Where do you stand? | 33 |
| Al-Quds | 37 |
| Dust | 39 |
| Enlightenment from nature | 41 |
| Just another pilgrim | 43 |
| The praiseworthy one | 45 |
| Syria | 47 |
| Palestine | 49 |
| Generation tech | 51 |
| A book | 53 |
| The purpose of being | 55 |
| Tears | 57 |

| | |
|---|---:|
| You and time | 59 |
| Fear | 61 |
| Race | 63 |
| Sleep | 65 |
| The Rohingya | 67 |
| Peace | 69 |
| Community | 71 |
| Greta sounds the alarm | 73 |
| Sheep | 75 |
| Capitalism | 77 |
| What you were given | 79 |
| War no more | 81 |
| You matter | 83 |
| Life | 85 |
| | |
| Glossary | 87 |
| Biographies of the quoted | 91 |
| Appendices | 99 |
| Bibliography | 105 |
| Notes | 111 |
| About the author | 117 |

# Preface

Being a refugee is not a crime. Being an immigrant is not a crime. Unfortunately, many Westerners don't seem to understand these experiences, and they tend to describe these arduous journeys as some foreign people leaving their countries in order to escape from their own problems, and then take "our" jobs, thereby becoming a burden to our systems. Some claim this is done for reasons of chain migration to the West, and even worse, others allege that refugees and/or immigrants fundamentally alter Western Christian civilization (i.e., the White race). Not surprisingly, during the Syrian refugee crisis which began in 2011, many conservative American politicians portrayed the Syrian refugees not as victims of a bloody civil war but as "terrorist suspects" who might be planning to attack Europe and the United States. These narratives and others persist up to the present moment. It is little wonder that asylum seekers at the southern border of the United States, many of whom were children, were often treated in very inhumane ways?

I will never forget the images of Afghan civilians running after the departing airplanes with Western personnel in the wake of the recent (2021) Taliban take-over of the country. I am certain these individuals did not want to leave their homes and families and risk their lives by clinging onto airplanes as they took off, but these acts tell of people's desperation to flee the country out of fear of persecution, hunger, or even death. During such desperate moments, people are only thinking of survival—not unemployment benefits, food vouchers, or other welfare assistance but survival. They simply have no other choice but to flee their most beloved of places and the communities they grew up in.

I am aware of these conservative concerns in the West, and undoubtedly some of these aforementioned allegations do materialize at times. However, those who take advantage of our systems, break laws, and the like, can be anyone—refugee, immigrant, or someone whose ancestors arrived on the Mayflower. As my family and I moved from one country to another, one refugee camp to another, the only thing on my mind was where we would be spending that night and if we were going to be safe when we woke up the next morning. We did this while wondering what might have happened to the rest of the family members back home, and if we would ever be able to return home again.

We must stop portraying immigrants and refugees as a threat. Most are victims of circumstances like violence, corruption, and starvation, which are becoming commonplace today. Some displaced people have no place to call home;

others would have remained in their homeland had Western colonial powers not plundered their resources, or intervened in their affairs in the first place.

Not every refugee or immigrant is the same and their experiences can differ vastly from one another, but what they all have in common, including with you and me, is that they want a life free of persecution, and fear. That should not be viewed as a crime. The Prophet Muhammad *pbuh* was himself a refugee, as were Abraham, Moses, and even the family of Jesus, among other prophets. How we respond to any refugee crisis says a lot about the rest of us who are currently not going through this suffering; it speaks volumes about our character and our humanity. To emphasize the magnitude of this matter, the Prophet Muhammad *pbuh* once said, "There is no leader who closes the door on someone in need or one suffering in poverty except that God closes the gates of the Heavens during his time of need."[2]

This collection of poems and reminders is dedicated to those individuals who have had to leave everything in search of a better future for themselves, their families, and their communities. I want to remember them! I hope you do too.

# A note from the author

It has been years since I published my last collection of poems, and I have not been a very active poet since then. I cannot explain why that is but I suspect it has to do with my work in academia and my PhD studies. My recent reading and writing have been professional in nature, and that has taken me away from the musical, idiosyncratic and associative language of poetry. I do not think I will ever grow fond of the dry, expository writing style, but that is where I currently stand.

This collection of poems is inspired by the 21st-century challenges we all face, as it attempts to outline many of them and where possible recommends desirable and/or available cures. It includes my latest poems as well as some of my favorite lines which I have previously published in various newspapers, books, and websites. It also contains some of the most beautiful lines of Muslim poetry and prose from 7th-century poets like Hassan ibn Thabit and al-Khansa to present-day poets like Burhan al-Din Fili, Joel Hayward, and Yahiya Emerick.

The excerpts of verses from other poets quoted in this book are some of my favorite selections of poetry, and I have included them in this collection to serve as references and daily reminders for readers, including myself. My poems in no way attempt to match those verses, but instead draw inspiration from the works of those remarkable individuals who have greatly influenced my thoughts and writing. The verses within represent my efforts to capture moments in time that have shaped my life thus far. Many of them have helped me find peace and healing on my life journey as a refugee of war and an immigrant. I hope you enjoy these humble verses as much as I did when I assembled them in one brief collection.

*"The full moon has risen over us*
*From the valley of Wadah*
*Now we owe it to show gratitude*
*So long as we call upon God.*
*O you raised among us*
*Coming with encouragement to be heeded*
*You have brought to this city nobleness*
*Welcome you, o caller to the best of ways."*[3]

— Traditional Islamic poem

# Introduction

Flamur Vehapi's work draws on the venerable tradition of Albanian poetry, one that links a bold directness of speech with a sweetness of cadence and an adroit turn of phrase. Informed by Persian and Turkish sensibilities, this tradition comfortably marries spiritual longing and religious identity with the highest aesthetic experience. Vehapi's poetry, in its style and idiom, recalls Albania's national poet Naim Frashëri as well as more recent voices like Arian Leka. However, these are poems written in English, drawing their music from the sounds, rhythms, and cadences of the English language, but in Vehapi's capable hands, such elements are shaped through a poetic practice that infuses his lyrics with a unique and refreshing expressiveness.

David Jalajel, poet, and author of
"A Short History of the Ghazal"

*"Not all a man hopes for does he attain -
the winds may blow in ways the ships do not desire."*[4]

— Al-Mutanabbi

## Our humanity

Times are trying,
Full of uncertainties.

Yesterday
I was deceived,
Today
I am heedless,
Tomorrow
Maybe I'll be lost
In the web of time
Tangled in confusion
In this world of illusion.

All you can do
Is stand upright.

No matter what tomorrow brings,
Struggle
To preserve your humanity.

Being human is a gift –
Discarding your humanity
Is a choice.

*"O God, the stars are shining;*
*All eyes have closed in sleep:*
*The kings have locked their doors.*
*Each lover is alone, in secret, with the one he loves.*
*And I am here too: alone, hidden from all of them— With You."*[5]

— Rabia al-Adawiyya

**Enough**

We
(You and I)
And most of
Our ancestors
Have experimented
With all that there is.

We
Pillaged
The resources of our planet –
We destroyed our world
For a few cents.

We killed animals
And harvested
Their organs
So that we
Can live
A comfortable
And luxurious life.

We even hurt
Each other
To meet our needs,
And when those needs were met,
We did it again
Because we could.

And worse –
We learned nothing
From all of this.
As the world around us crumbles
We go about our business
As if all is fine.

Think –
What kind of world did we find,
And what kind of world
Are we leaving behind?

O children of Adam...
What will our legacy be?


"...*For anyone who does not taste the bitterness*
*of acquiring knowledge,*
*he will taste the humiliation of ignorance all his life.*"[6]

— Imam al-Shafi'i

## COVID-19

It hit us
As if out of the blue,
But it is nothing new.

It closed in on us,
Socially distanced us,
Confounded us and caused a lot of fuss.

We were too cozy
In our little worlds, our own bubbles,
Too distant from fear and troubles.

It silently knocked on our doors
And brought many to their senses,
Made them question their worldly inferences.

Others went about their days,
With no precautions or care.
It is all a hoax, they haughtily declared.

We usually pride ourselves
In our achievements and technology,
But we proved no match for this tiny enemy.
It followed us down the streets, into stores,

Made us run from our own shadows,
Not to mention family, friends, and foes.

What I fear is not
Whether this affliction will go away or lessen,
But we'll come out of it not learning a single lesson.

> *"Be generous, my eyes, with shedding copious tears*
> *and weep a stream of tears for Sakhr![7]*
> *I could not sleep and was awake all night...*
> *I watched the stars, though it was not my task to watch;*
> *at times I wrapped myself in my remaining rags...*
> *He would protect his comrade in a fight, a match*
> *for those who fight with weapons, tooth, or claw*
> *Amidst a troupe of horses straining at their bridles eagerly,*
> *like lions that arrive in pastures lush."[8]*

— Al-Khansa

## Where do you stand?

Tyrants and fear-mongers
have been roaming around
Since our beginning.

They have destroyed lives
And oppressed people,
And one thing is certain:
They also left one day,
Only to be replaced
With new ones.

They are villains and despots
But what are you? A silent bystander?
Know that your dismal silence
Does not end the suffering of the oppressed,
It only gives the green light to the oppressor.

Today,
While the tormentors
Commit their crimes,
You stand there,
A hopeless spectator,
Watching children cry for help,
And others dying in agony.
Don't just stand there,

Do something now!
If you cannot change
With your hands,
Said the Prophet,
Then change it with your tongue,
And if not that
At least change it with your heart.⁹

> *"I see the world has many ills,*
> *its dweller sickens, then he dies.*
> *Good friends meet then separate -*
> *but short of death, all this is small.*
> *I lose a friend and then one more,*
> *sure proof that none on Earth abide."*¹⁰

— Ali Ibn Abi Talib

## A strange case

Strange is the case
Of our brothers and sisters.

They walk the earth
As if they own it all,
Every inch of it!

But what do they really own?
Their wealth? Their homes?
Their clothes, maybe?
How about their bodies?
Or their souls?

Ah, none of those.
If they gave it some thought,
They would clearly see
That they really own nothing
And I mean nothing at all!

They'll leave this world
Just as they entered it
Decades ago –
Naked,
Without even a scrap of cloth
To cover their privates.

Welcome to the world!
Hope you made some preparations
For your onward journey
Today,
Or tomorrow.[11]


*"Do not be distressed by the disasters that always strike ...
the calamities of this world are not permanent."*[12]

— Imam al-Shafi'i

## Al-Quds

You have been there
Since time began.
You have seen
What no one else has seen.
You have been occupied
And you have been freed.
You have lived
Through it all
But have never lost hope,
Never ceased to be.
Your smiles never faded
And never stopped
Conquering hearts
Across the world.

These sad oppressors,
Will one day resign in despair
Like so many who came before,
But you will remain
As you always have
For centuries to come,
A place for all people,
A place for many faiths,
United under the Creator
Of all.

*"I would rather be enslaved by the Power I cannot see than be deceived by a walking dust like me!"*[3]

— Burhan Al-Din Fili

## Dust

I am
Nothing more
Than unsettled dust
From the past
Shaped into a human form,
Frozen in time,
And waiting
For the divine breeze
To blow me away –
Away from this world,
This world of dust;
To blow my inner self
Back to its Creator,
When and only when
Its time is up.
For now,
I am thankful
To be who – and what –
I am.[14]

*"Ah God, what a river! It flows in the valley,
a watering place lovelier than a girl's crimson lips,
As it bends like a bracelet; flanked by flowers
It resembles the Milky Way."*[5]

— Ibn Khafajah

## Enlightenment from nature

The world is full of lessons –
Everywhere you look
You see a teacher.
Everything you hear
Speaks a message.
Whatever you touch
Shares its secret.

Nature imparts its wisdom
To those who listen.

Right now,
As the stream flows
And the pebbles skitter
Through the pure water,
There is a calming sound
That teaches peace
To our hearts.[16]

*"And more excellent than you, my eye has never seen,
And more beautiful than you, no woman ever gave birth to;
You were created free from any flaw whatsoever,
As though you were created just the way you wanted."*[7]

— Hassan ibn Thabit

## Just another pilgrim

Waking up in the morning
Realizing I'm still alive,
I gratefully start the day
Like a bee starts from its hive.
Jumping from flower to flower
In search of truth and light,
Seeking the nectar of knowledge
Until the dead of night.
Hoping to live this life
As humbly as I can,
Knowing that in this world
A pilgrim is all I am.[18]

*"By God, no woman has conceived and born  
One like the apostle, the prophet of mercy and the guide*

*Nor has there walked on the surface of the earth  
One more faithful to the protection of a neighbor  
or to a promise*

*Than he who was the light that shone on us  
Blessed in his deeds, just, and rightly guided."*[9]

— Hassan ibn Thabit

## The praiseworthy one

Among dunes, in a land
Long forgotten by the world,
The praiseworthy one was born
In the Year of the Elephant
By the decree of his Lord.

And there he was raised
An orphan. Little could he imagine
How much he would be praised.

At forty, the age of maturity,
He sought to dispel his heart's gloom.
The Almighty granted him
The greatest responsibility,
Entrusting him with His final torch
To illuminate the world
For all humanity.

This was no easy task
For him or his followers,
But he never complained,
And to fulfill his mission
He remained
Strong and determined.

After years of hardship –
Of pressure, hunger, and torture,
His message of peace, for justice
And forgiveness, captured
Even the hearts of his foes.

From a forgotten land,
Through sacrifice and pain,
He came out triumphant.
Because of who he was
And what he had done
For his people, he
Will always remain
The praiseworthy one.[20]

> *"Time is only as such,*
> *face it with patience,*
> *the calamity is on wealth*
> *or a separation from a loved one."*[21]

— Imam al-Shafi'i

## Syria

It is a name
Heavy with meaning –
History
And deep emotions
Saturate it.
They drip
From every letter
Of the word.

A civilization
Born of struggle,
Built on faith,
Progress,
Respect,
And communal love.

Now,
Those same letters weep –
There is suffering,
Neglect,
Degradation,
Disregard for human life,
Lives of people
Like you and I.

Tears and blood
Fuse together.
They flow
From the pages
Of our sorrowful history –
A tome that reads: The World Has Failed Us,
And So Have You.




*"Let me free so that like the Sun I shall wear a robe of fire,
And within that fire like a Sun to adorn the world."*[22]

— Jalal al-Din Muhammad Rumi

## Palestine

A land washed in blood,
Where rocks turn to dust
And dust is blown away
By the uncaring
Winds of time –
Where flowers keep growing
No matter the terror
And the oppressors
Of the age.

Palestine,
You have seen
More than any eyes can bear,
But no matter the hardships
And the struggles,
You just won't surrender,
You just won't resign
Though you burn in flame –
You're Palestine.

*"I am a spirit, and this is naught but flesh,*
*It was my abode and my garment for a time.*
*I am a treasure, by a talisman kept hid,*
*Fashioned of dust, which served me as a shrine,*
*I am a pearl, which has left its shell deserted,*
*I am a bird, and this body was my cage,*
*Whence I have now flown forth and it is left as a token,*
*Praise to God, who hath now set me free…"*[23]

— Abu Hamid al-Ghazali

## Generation tech

People –
Men, women, and children,
Young and old,
From all backgrounds
And all corners
Of the globe
Are "coming together"
In one place,
At the same time,
"Connected"
With devices
Glued to their faces.

They are busy
"Communicating"
Behind a screen,
Alone,
In a world
Full of people
Waiting to be discovered,
To be seen and heard,
To be cared for,
To be cherished,
Company
To be enjoyed.

Reality is no longer
Real and exciting
To them,
No longer relevant,
So one gets a
Machine
To be validated,
To make them happy,
To make them human.

To me
It seems like
We have disconnected
From life itself!

*"Time is to be used wisely
because life is made up of time itself."*[24]

— Sami Frashëri

## A book

A book
Home of the letters,
Crate of ideas, thoughts,
And experiences of the past,
An open ocean.

A world of learning,
Peace and comfort
In the hands of the reader
Is barely clinging
To the branches
Of dying trees.

Once a revolutionary force
To be reckoned with
And a yearned-for commodity,
Now just another artifact
In the rusty shelves
Of a people-empty library.

If you are looking for a motivator,
It has already been given to you,
It is, in fact, a command:
*Iqra!*[25]

*"My peace, brothers, is in my aloneness
Because my Beloved is alone with me there—always.
I've found nothing to equal His love,
That Love which harrows the sands of my desert.
If I die of desire, and He is still unsatisfied—
That sorrow has no end."*[26]

— Rabia al Adawiyya

# The purpose of being

I am here
For a few numbered days –
Yesterday I was little,
Now I am of age.
As for tomorrow,
I don't really know
If I will be here,
Or if there will even be
A tomorrow…

I am here,
To live this life
And enjoy it
To the fullest,
In submission,
But I refuse to waste
A second of it
In idle talk,
Or get involved
In useless doings.

Dear well-wisher,
If you are one of these people
Please make way for me.
I have a long journey
To prepare for,
And you and I
Have never met.

*"If my Lord would kindly grant it,
I would go there, weeping, weeping,
And Muhammad in Madinah
I would see there, weeping, weeping."*[27]

— Yunus Emre

**Tears**

There is no shame
In shedding worthy tears.

Cry
When the heart is tearful,
Laugh
When it is light.

If your Creator
Is pleased with you,
It makes no difference
What people say
Or think of you.

Tears are a mercy.
When the heart hardens,
The eyes run dry.[28]

*"Seek the wisdom
of a sage,
The knowledge
of a scholar,
The strength
of a warrior,
And the love
Of a mother."*[29]

— Yahiya Emerick

## You and time

Time has been,
Is,
And will be, here –
But you and I
Have not been,
And we will not be here
For long.

We are here
Today,
But soon
We'll be preparing
To go,
Leaving this world
Like we came.
With nothing.

Truly,
We are all at loss,
Except for those of us
Who use time
Mindfully,
And advise each other
To goodness, to patience,
And to truth![30]

*"Allah is the great silence
the unconquerable quietness*

*inside and beyond a universe that creaks
moans and shrieks*

*Emptiness obeyed a single word, "be"
and became an impenetrable fullness…"*[31]

— Joel Hayward

**Fear**

We fear the unknown –
And the known.
We fear death
And we fear life.
Some of us fear poverty.
Some even fear wealth.
There are those who fear others,
And many others
Fear themselves.

Most of us
Live a life of fear,
But a life of fear
Is no life at all.

Fear will bind you up
And drown you
In the darkest ocean.
So let it go
And be free –
Make fear
Fear you!

*"With love I convert the crude copper I have into gold,
For when I meet You tomorrow, You will want a gift from me."*[32]

— Muhammad Iqbal

## Race

A label,
A social construct,
A box –
Check!
An inhuman myth
To dominate
And oppress
People,
Like you
And me.

A label,
An excuse
To hold on to power.

A tool
To divide and conquer.
A crime.

All of us
Come from
Adam,
And Adam
Was from dust.[33]

*"Love is the spice of life,
without love life has no taste."*[34]

— Sami Frashëri

## Sleep

Dear friend,
Lover of sleep,
Take that nap.
Yes, get some rest.
But keep in mind
That so very soon
You will go back to sleep
One final time,
For eternity.

If I were you
I'd sleep less
And ponder more.

Isn't is a shame
That birds
Start their day
Before most of us start ours?[35]

*"O shining moon,*
*We are so different from each other!*
*The heart that feels pain*
*Is a different heart indeed.*
*Yet you are far removed from the station of awareness.*
*I know the purpose of my life -*
*And this is a radiance your face does not have."*[36]

— Muhammad Iqbal

# The Rohingya

A people
Stronger than mountains
Are pushed by fire and wind –

Scattered
From land to land,
Hoping for help
And for peace.
Their tears
Flow to our doorsteps,
But we step over
Their cries.

Surely,
After every difficulty,
There will be ease.

*"Thee I choose, of all the world alone;*
*Wilt thou suffer me to sit in grief?*
*My heart is a pen in thy hand,*
*Thou art the cause if I am glad or melancholy…*
*Thou wert first, and last thou shalt be;*
*Make my last better than my first…*
*I have nothing, except thou hast bestowed it."*[37]

— Jalal al-Din Muhammad Rumi

**Peace**

A feeling
Sought by most,
Enjoyed
By few.

A word
Thrown around,
Used left and right
But hardly centered
Or understood.

Peace is not bestowed;
It is attained
By those
Who are mindful
Of how it surrounds them.

Peace was here,
But where were you?
It will be there –
Where will you be?

*"If you—the spiritual aspirant—realize your attributes of servitude,
you will then be assisted with something of the attributes of the Eternally Besought.*

*Realize your abject character and impoverishment, and you will gain dignity and wealth from the All-Powerful."*[38]

— Imam al-Mawlud

## Community

Community is dying,
There is no denying.

We have big houses
With empty rooms.
We have built walls
And forgot the doors.

We have plenty of resources,
So one overeats
While the rest go hungry.

We know that people
Need our help,
But we are too busy
Staring at screens,
Or too tired
From the previous night's
Party.

Yes, we have friends,
Hundreds of them,
In our devices
But none by our side
When we need them
Because we were not there
When they needed us.

People talk to their pets
But not to their neighbours;
I'm sure there's a universe somewhere
Where people find that strange.

There is no denying
Our communities are dying.

> "O Lord, free the intellect from slavery,
> And make the young teachers of their elders;
> Bestow on them the power to pulsate with life,
> The Heart of Ali and the love of Siddiq..."[39]

— Muhammad Iqbal

## Greta sounds the alarm

A 15-year-old
Sounds the alarm –
A bell rings out
To wake us up
From somnolence to hope.

A child is hailing us
As our boat sinks.
Our oceans rise
And our lands burn,
But most of us
Roll over in sleep
Or close our eyes tighter,
Hoping it's a dream.

One young soul
Organizes a strike
For climate action.
Fast forward a year –
There's a global faction.

Do not underestimate
The power of one.
Heed the bell.
Don't die in your sleep.[40]

*"If you ventured in pursuit of glory,
don't be satisfied with less than the stars."*[41]

— al-Mutanabbi

## Sheep

People,
Our brothers and sisters,
Like sheep,
Fall for it all.

A new egomaniac
Utters the same message
With the same words
And they flock to it.

Every time.
And when their favorite liar
Is exposed,
They jump hoops
To justify his stupidity
Or whitewash
His fascist drivel.
Or both.

All it takes
To herd them
Around you
Is to pull a new lie
Out of the same old sack
Of trusty deception
And you have a following
Of sheep.

*"Planet Earth can feed every one of us,
But most of the resources that come from it
Are wasted and spent recklessly;
As a result, many are forced to go hungry."*[42]

— Sami Frashëri

## Capitalism

Capitalism
We assembled a lie,
And now we believe it.

We built a monster
And it's out of control.

Capitalism is the reality
That snatches the only morsel of food
Out of the mouths of the poor
And feeds it to the wealthy,
Although the wealthy
Have full bellies.

For us to survive,
The monster must die.

*"You know you're no more than a passing glance,*
*Yet your sacred duty is yourself to enhance.*
*Behold the winds of life so bitterly blow,*
*It's not in your power to change its flow.*
*Lo, what is meant to be you cannot negate,*
*Through its wilderness you must navigate.*
*Don't take life for granted, but cherish it.*
*In the midst of darkness the candles of hope are lit.*
*The Creator of life you worship and adore,*
*You're created to be a star, not a burning meteor."*[43]

— Burhan Al-Din Fili

# What you were given

You were given treasures:
Body, soul and life,
So many treasures,
Too many to count.

You were given treasures,
Wealth being one,
And when you had the chance to help
Those needier than you,
Did you respond!

You were given it all,
But what have you done?!
It's the giving that enriches you,
Not the keeping.

Drop everything now –
Emulate
Abu Bakr as-Siddiq!

*"The station of love is beyond the reach of Your angels,
Only those with dauntless courage are up to it."*⁴⁴

— Muhammad Iqbal

## War no more

War –
They said:
It is the answer;
A means to an end…

War –
They lamented:
Bloodshed is the way
To a solution.
Nonsense.

War –
It starts
When reason ends;
A tragic end.

War –
There is nothing glorious
Where it leads.

War –
You want glory?
Die a hero
Preventing it.

*"O God, the stars are shining;*
*All eyes have closed in sleep:*
*The kings have locked their doors.*
*Each lover is alone, in secret, with the one he loves.*
*And I am here too: alone, hidden*
*from all of them— With You."*[45]

— Rabia al-Adawiyya

## You matter

Yes,
You are one person
In a crowd of billions,
But you still matter.

You are one person
In this great span of time,
Yet you still matter.

Yes,
You are one person
In this vast universe,
And you still matter.

No matter who tries
To belittle you,
And put you down,
Don't heed them,
Because you matter.

You wouldn't be here
If you didn't!

*"... the lucky stars set at the sight.
They hid kindness, knowledge and mercy
The night they laid him unpillowed in the dust
And went away in sorrow without their prophet…
Can any day the dead is mourned
Equal the morning of the day Muhammad died?
On which the seat of revelation was taken from them
Which had been a source of light everywhere."*[46]

— Hassan ibn Thabit

**Life**

God-given beauty
To all who breathe,
Have eyes to see,
And minds to contemplate.

A passing glimpse
Full of charm,
Temptation and play.

Yet it is a fading shadow,
Deceiving
Those who cling to it.

I'll pack for this life lightly
Taking only what I need.
No point
Weighing myself down,
Because one day soon,
At journey's end,
I'll leave it all.

*"A small book
with the fragrance
of freshly turned soil
the spark of the Big Bang
the sweat of humanity*

*calls and weeps*

*Forests and deliverance
spring up where
the
drops
fall
all in Arabic…"*[47]

— Joel Hayward

# Glossary

**Adhan:** The Islamic call to prayer. It is made five times a day, ordinarily from the minarets of mosques, to remind Muslims that it is time to pray

**AH:** "Anno Hegirae" is used to denote the Islamic calendar that starts from the *hijrah* in 623 CE

**Alhamdulillah:** An Arabic phrase of thanks and devotion: "Praise be to God"

**Allah:** Arabic word for God

**Allahu Akbar**: Islamic phrase: "God is the Greatest/Supreme!"

**BCE:** "Before the Common Era" is used in place of BC to denote a Gregoian year

**Caliph/Khalifah:** Successor (to the Prophet Muhammad *pbuh*); a supreme religious and political leader of an Islamic political entity known as a caliphate

**CE:** "Common Era" is used in place of AD to denote a Gregorian year

**Fitrah:** The pure and original human nature as created by God and with which every human being is born

**Ghazal:** a lyric poem with repeated rhyme and a fixed number of verses (common in Arabic literature as well as other cultures)

**Hadith:** Written narrative reports of Prophet Muhammad's *pbuh* sayings, actions and approvals

**Hijrah:** "Emigration" refers to the journey of the Prophet *pbuh* from Makkah to Madinah, and it also marks the beginning of the Islamic calendar

**Imam:** Arabic for "leader"; ordinarily given to the person who leads prayer in a mosque

**Iman:** The concept of faith consisting of belief in God, the angels, the books of God, the prophets, predestination, the Prophet Muhammad *pbuh* and the Day of Judgment

**Insha'Allah:** An Islamic phrase: "God willing" or "if God wills"

**Iqra:** "Read," "recite" or "relate" was the first revealed word of the Qur'an to the Prophet *pbuh*

**Islam:** Submission to the will of God alone

**Jihad:** Arabic for "struggle" or "effort"

**Kabah:** The Sacred House of God in Makkah; the holiest site in Islam

**Madinah:** The shortened form of Madinah-tun Nabi – the City of the Prophet Muhammad *pbuh*, formerly known as Yathrib

**Makkah:** The birthplace of Prophet Muhammad *pbuh*; the location of the Kabah

**Nasheed:** Islamic chants; vocal music

**Pbuh:** Short for "peace be upon him" used after the names of the prophets

**Qasidah**: The "golden odes" of Arabic; a laudatory, elegiac, or satiric poem that is found in Arabic literature, among other cultures

**Qur'an:** Islam's divine scripture

**Quraysh:** The tribe of the Prophet Muhammad *pbuh*

**Sadaqah:** Charity

**Shahadah:** Profession of faith: "There is no god but Allah and Muhammad is His final messenger" (the first pillar of Islam)

**Shariah:** Legal tradition, Islamic law or "path"; rules and regulations that govern the day-to-day life of Muslims

**Sunnah:** Traditions (sayings, actions, and approvals) of the Prophet Muhammad *pbuh*

**Ummah:** The Muslim community; community of the faithful

**Zakat:** the obligatory charity tax on every Muslim

# Biographies of the quoted

**Hassan ibn Thabit (563-674)** was an Arab poet from Madinah, and a companion of the Prophet Muhammad *pbuh*. Thabit is best known for his poems dedicated to the Prophet Muhammad. Prior to the advent of Islam, he won acclaim at the courts of various Christian Arab kings in the region, but right after the appearance of Prophet Muhammad, Thabit accepted Islam at the age of sixty and is said to have become the first poetic defender of Islam and the Prophet Muhammad. It is also said that his poems were instrumental in spreading the message of the new prophet in the region since poetry was an essential part of Arab culture. To this day, the works of Thabit are regarded as the most beautiful of lines in praise of the Prophet Muhammad.[48]

**Al-Khansa (575-645)**, whose real name was Tamadir bint Amr, is one of the most famous female poets of the Arab world. She is said to have converted to Islam during the time of Prophet Muhammad *pbuh*, and her masterpieces are eulogies dedicated to her two brothers killed during pre-Islamic times (one of her brothers was Sakhr, who is mentioned in the poem cited in this book). During her time, she is said to have appeared at different poetry contests in Makkah and the region. Many of Al-Khansa's verses were collected and reintroduced by Ibn al-Sikkit (802–858), a writer from the early Abbasid era.[49]

**Ali ibn Abi Talib (600-661)**, born in Makkah, is commonly known as the cousin of Prophet Muhammad *pbuh* and the fourth of the *Rashidun* caliphs. Having been raised in the household of the Prophet himself, Ali was the first child to accept Islam. The young convert to the faith was by the Prophet's side from his childhood to the time of the Prophet's passing in 632 CE. Ali was an exceptionally devout person, wise beyond his years, and one of the bravest in the battlefield. In addition to being a commander and state leader, among other things, he was also a prolific poet. Because of his many great personal qualities and commitment to Islam, he was known by names like "the lion of God," "the gate of knowledge," and the like. Ali married the daughter of the Prophet, Fatimah al-Zahra, and it was their offspring who carried on the lineage of the Prophet Muhammad. After the passing of the Prophet, Ali focused mainly on his devotion to God and serving his family and the community, although he was also a trusted adviser to all previous caliphs: Abu Bakr, Omar and Uthman. When the assassination of Uthman took place, however, the Muslim council chose Ali as the fourth caliph of Islam. Ali reigned from 656 to 661, ruling a vast empire. Ali was assassinated in the city of Kufah, present-day Iraq, and with his passing the great *Rashidun Caliphate* period came to an end.[50]

**Rabia al-Adawiyya (717-801)** who is also known as Rabia al-Basri was a poet from Basra, Iraq, and lived during the Islamic Golden Age. She is known throughout the Muslim world for her piety and asceticism, as well as her eloquent verses on Divine beauty and love. She is said to have been influenced by the teachings of Hassan al-Basri (641-728), who was one of the most prominent religious figures in early Islam. Most of the information we have about al-Adawiyya's life and work came to us through the writings of Farid ud-Din Attar (1145 – 1221).[51]

**Imam Shafi'i (767-819)** whose full name was Muhammad ibn Idris ibn al-'Abbas bin Uthman bin Shafi bin al-Saib bin Ubayd bin Abd Yazid bin Hashim bin Abd al-Muttalib bin Abd Manaf was a theologian, writer, and scholar, often referred to as 'Shaykh al-Islam.' He descended from the Bani Hashim tribe and traced his lineage back to Prophet Muhammad *pbuh*. He was born in Gaza, Palestine, but lived and worked in Makkah, Madinah, Yemen, Iraq and Egypt. He authored more than 100 books and is known to have created the essentials of the science of fiqh (the system of Islamic jurisprudence). Imam Shafi'i passed away in Egypt at the age of 54.[52]

**Al-Mutanabbi (915-965)** was originally from Kufah, Iraq, and lived during the Abbasid period. Although primarily a composer of panegyrics, he is regarded by many as the greatest poet of the Arabic language. Other topics he wrote about were philosophy, courage, leadership, description of battles, and the like. His great poetic style combined with his social and networking skills are said to have earned him great popularity at royal courts and life in general.[53]

**Abu Hamid Muhammad al-Ghazali (1058-1111)** was as one of the most prominent spiritual scholars of his time. Born in Tus (in present-day Iran), he was a polymath in every sense of the word. So influential was he that many Muslims referred to him as a "renewer of the faith" (someone who appears once every century to revive the faith of the community, according to hadith traditions). Although he authored numerous books, his greatest work, based on personal religious experiences, is *Ihya ulum al-din*. In it, al-Ghazali explained the foundations and the practices of Islam, and showed how these teachings can be made the basis of a profound reverential life. No matter the time or place, Al-Ghazali's writings are an inspiration to Muslims worldwide.[54]

**Abu Ishaq ibn Ibrahim ibn Abu al-Fath (1058-1139)**, also known as Ibn Khafajah**,** was one of the most famous poets of Andalusia during the period of Almoravid dynasty. He was born in Alzira, a city near Valencia (in present-day Spain), and that is where he spent most of his life. Ibn Khafajah was famous for his nature poetry, in which he humanized the environment.[55]

**Jalal al-Din Muhammad Rumi (1207-1273)**, better known to us as Rumi, was one of the most prominent poets and religious figures of his time. Born and educated in Balkh (now in Afghanistan), at an early age Rumi and his family were forced to leave their lands due to Mongol invasions in the region and settled in Konya (now in Turkey). Through his eloquent use of Persian, his native language, as well as Arabic and Turkish, Rumi's writings and message slowly reached all corners of the Muslim world. In the 20th century, Rumi's works began to widely circulate in Europe and the Americas. Today he is known as America's best-selling poet but that has come at a cost since, for various reasons, his original message has been greatly misinterpreted and misunderstood,[56] and in order to appease the Western audience, his faith is subtly erased in many translations of his writings.[57]

**Yunus Emre (1238-1328)** was a pre-Ottoman Turkish folk poet and religious leader from Anatolia. His writings and teachings, written in Old Anatolian Turkish, were mostly about Divine love and human destiny, characterized by deep feelings and thought. His work is said to have greatly influenced Turkish culture and literature, and continues to inspire people to this present moment.

**Sami Frashëri (1850-1904)** was born into a distinguished Muslim family in the District of Përmet in Albania (then under Ottoman rule). He attended a Greek language school in Janina, and it was there that he became proficient in French, Italian and Greek, and later learned Arabic, Persian and Turkish, in addition to his native Albanian. After moving to Istanbul, Frashëri worked for several Ottoman newspapers, and also published over fifty of his own books in a number of languages on a variety of subjects and genres. Recently, Frashëri was recognized as one of the great Muslims of the West for his contributions to Islamic civilization.[58]

**Imam Muḥammad al-Mawlud (1844-1905)** was born in Mauritania, West Africa. He, like many others in his family, came from a long line of scholars who were also accomplished writers and religious scholars and ran traditional Islamic schools. From an early age, al-Mawlud became a student of the Qur'an, and later he studied jurisprudence, *fiqh*, grammar, and other sciences related to the Arabic language. Soon, students from around the country flocked to al-Mawlud's teaching/learning circles. He authored over 70 works.[59]

**Muhammad Iqbal (1877-1938)** was a South Asian Muslim philosopher, poet, and politician of the highest caliber. His poetry in Urdu, his native language, is considered the greatest of the 20th century. Born and raised in Punjab (present-day Pakistan), Iqbal studied in his native lands and later in England and Germany. As an influential politician, he was a strong proponent for a separate state for the Muslims in British-ruled India, and many of his works and visions later gave birth to the state of Pakistan. Today, he is a spiritual inspiration for many Muslims across the world.[60]

**Burhan Al-Din Fili (1949-)** was born in Koplik, Albania. At the time, Albania was under strict Communist rule, which made the country prison-like. The young poet was left with no choice but to break free. In 1976 he swam across Lake Shkodra reaching former Yugoslavia where he was caught, jailed and interrogated. After a time, he escaped to Italy where he spent months in a refugee camp. In 1977 he moved to the United States, and in 1982 he went to Egypt where he attended Al-Azhar University. After the collapse of Communism in 1991, he returned to Albania and contributed to the democratic life of his people. Currently involved in international humanitarian work, Fili is a scholar, poet, and lover of knowledge and books.[61]

**Joel Hayward (1964-)** is a New Zealand scholar, writer and poet who has held various academic posts, including Chair of the Department of Humanities and Social Sciences at Khalifa University (UAE) and Dean of the Royal Air Force College (UK). He has earned *ijazas* in ʿAqīdah (theology) and Sirah (the Prophet's biography). He is the author or editor of many books of nonfiction, particularly in the fields of history and strategic studies. He has given strategic advice to political and military leaders in several countries, has given policy and religious advice to prominent sheikhs, and was tutor to His Royal Highness Prince William of Wales.[62]

**Yahiya Emerick** is an American convert to Islam who has been involved in interfaith issues and education since 1990. He has since become an internationally recognized author, lecturer, and educator. He has a graduate degree in history, has authored numerous books for adults and children, mostly fiction, and has been published in many reputable magazines, including the Journal for Religion and Education. One of Emerick's books was adopted into the curriculum of Al-Azhar University, known today as the most respected university for Islamic learning.

# Appendices

## A: Selected Qur'anic Verses

*Surah (Chapter) 1, Verse 1-7:*
Praise be to Allah, Lord of the Worlds,
The Beneficent, the Merciful.
Owner of the Day of Judgment,
Thee (alone) we worship; Thee (alone) we ask for help.
Show us the straight path,
The path of those whom Thou hast favoured. Not (the path) of those who earn Thine anger nor of those who go astray.

*Surah 2, Verse 255:*
Allah! There is no God save Him, the Alive, the Eternal.
Neither slumber nor sleep overtaketh Him.
Unto Him belongeth whatsoever is in the heavens and whatsoever is in the earth.
Who is he that intercedeth with Him save by His leave?
He knoweth that which is in front of them and that which is

behind them, while they encompass nothing of His knowledge save what He will.

His throne includeth the heavens and the earth, and He is never weary of preserving them. He is the Sublime, the Tremendous.

*Surah 8, Verses 61-62:*
And if they incline to peace, incline thou also to it, and trust in Allah. Lo! He is the Hearer, the Knower.
And if they would deceive thee, then lo! Allah is Sufficient for thee.
He it is Who supporteth thee with His help and with the believers.

*Surah 29, Verse 46:*
And argue not with the People of the Scripture unless it be in (a way) that is better, save with such of them as do wrong; and say: We believe in that which hath been revealed unto us and revealed unto you; our God and your God is One, and unto Him we surrender.

*Surah 59, Verse 23:*
He is Allah, than Whom there is no other God,
the Sovereign Lord, the Holy One, Peace,
the Keeper of Faith, the Guardian, the Majestic,
the Compeller, the Superb. Glorified be Allah
from all that they ascribe as partners (unto Him).

*Surah 112:*
Say: He is Allah, the One!
Allah, the eternally Besought of all!
He begetteth not nor was begotten.
And there is none comparable unto Him.[63]

## B: Selected Hadith

Whosoever plants a tree and diligently looks after it until it matures and bears fruit is rewarded.

Every religion has a special character; and the characteristic of Islam is modesty.

Do you love God? Love your fellow beings first.

No man is a true believer unless he desires for his brother what he desires for himself.

God will not be merciful to those who are not merciful to people.

The servants of God are those who walk the earth in humility.

Kindness is a mark of faith; those without kindness are also without faith.

Have compassion on those who live on earth and He Who is in Heaven will have compassion on you.

The most excellent *jihad* is the conquest of one's ego.

Do not be angry.

A strong person is not he who throws his adversaries to the ground. A strong person is the one who contains himself when angry.

Strive always to excel in virtue and truth.

Say what is true, although it may be bitter and displeasing to people.

Doing justice is charity; and assisting a man upon his beast and lifting his baggage is charity, and pure, comforting words are charity … and removing that which is an inconvenience to wayfarer … is a charity.

Indeed, an ignorant man who is generous is dearer to God than a worshipper who is miserly.

Feed the hungry, and visit the sick … and assist the oppressed.

It is better for a leader to make a mistake in forgiving than to make a mistake in punishing.

Seek knowledge from the cradle to the grave.

An hour's contemplation is better than a year's worship.

He who knows himself knows God.[64]

# Bibliography

Abu al-Faadil, Rabiʻa. *Hassān ibn Thābit al-ansārī: shāʻir al-Islām*. Beirut: Dār al-ʻIlm lil-Malāyīn, 1993.

Al-Ghazali, Abu Hamid. *The Alchemy of Happiness*. Trans. and ed. Claud Field and Elton I. Daniel. London, M.E. Sharpe, 1991.

Ali, Rozina. "The Erasure of Islam from the Poetry of Rumi." *The New Yorker*, 5 Jan. 2017, www.newyorker.com/books/page-turner/the-erasure-of-islam-from-the-poetry-of-rumi.

*A Kaleidoscope of Stories : Muslim Voices in Contemporary Poetry*. Edited by R. S. Spiker, Cambridge, Lote Tree Press, 2020.

ʻArafat, Walid. "An Aspect of the Forger's Art in Early Islamic Poetry." *Bulletin of the School of Oriental and African Studies, University of London* 28, no. 3 (1965): 477-482.

Arberry, A. J., translator. *Poems of Al-Mutanabbi: A Selection with Introduction, Translations and Notes.* Cambridge, 1967.

Ashour, Radwa, et al., editors. *Arab Women Writers : A Critical Reference Guide, 1873-1999.* Translated by Mandy McClure, American University In Cairo Press, 2008.

al-Ghazzālī, Abu Hamid Muhammad. *Al-Ghazālī's Letter to a Disciple : Ayyula'l-Walad: Bilingual English-Arabic Edition Translated with an Introduction & Note.* Translated by Tobias Mayer, Islamic Texts, 2005.

Asani, Ali, and Kamal Abdel-Malek. *Celebrating Muhammad: Images of the Prophet in Popular Muslim Poetry.* University Of South Carolina Press, 1995.

al-Tūnisī , Muḥammad. *In Darfur: An Account of the Sultanate and Its People.* Translated by Humphrey Davies, NYU Press, 2020.

Boutz, Jennifer. *Hassan Ibn Thabit, a True Mukhadram: A Study of the Ghassanid Odes of Hassan Ibn Thabit.* 2009, pp. 1–261, repository.library.georgetown.edu/bitstream/handle/10822/557924/Boutz_georgetown_0076D_10357.pdf?sequence=1. Accessed 8 Aug. 2021.

Ciabattari, Jane. "Why Is Rumi the Best-Selling Poet in the US?" *Www.bbc.com*, 21 Oct. 2014, www.bbc.com/culture/article/20140414-americas-best-selling-poet.

Emerick, Yahiya. *In the Gardens of Delight*. Vol. 1, Amirah Publishing, 2021.

Frashëri, Sami. *The Album of Aphorisms*. Translated by Flamur Vehapi, EA, 2019.

Haider, Sajjad. "Iqbal and his philosophy." *Allamaiqbal.com*, allamaiqbal.com/publications/journals/review/apr68/1.htm. Accessed 19 Aug. 2021.

Harvey, Andrew, and Eryk Hanut. *Perfume of the Desert*. Theosophical Publishing, 1999.

Hayward, Joel S A. *Poems from the Straight Path : A Book of Islamic Verse*. Ashland, Oregon, White Cloud Press, 2017.

Ibn Salāmah Quḍāʿī, Muḥammad. *A Treasury of Virtues : Sayings, Sermons and Teachings of ʿAlī by Al-Qāḍī Al-Quḍāʾi : With the One Hundred Proverbs Attributed to Al-Jāhiẓ*. Translated by Tahera Qutbuddin, New York, New York University Press, 2016.

Ibn Hisham, Abd al-Mālik. *The Life of Muhammad : A Translation of Ishaq's Slrat Rasul Allah*. Translated by A Guillaume, London, Oxford Univ. Press, 1955.

Ibn Thabit, Hassan. *Diwan of Hassan Ibn Thabit*. Edited by Walid N. ⁧Arafat. E. J. W. Gibb Memorial Series. 2 vols. London: Luzac, 1971.

Imam al-Mawlud. *Purification of the Heart : Signs, Symptoms, and Cures of the Spiritual Diseases of the Heart : Translation and Commentary of Imam Mawlud's Matharat Al-Qulub*. Translated by Hamza Yusuf, Starlatch Books, 2004.

Iqbal, Muhammad. *Shikwa & Jawab Shikwa: The Complaint and the Answer*. Translated by Abdussalam Puthige, The Other Press, 2020.

Iqbal, Muhammad. *Tulip in the Desert : A Selection of the Poetry of Muhammad Iqbal*. Translated by Mustansir Mir, Mcgill Queen's University Press, 2000.

Ismail, Abdul Qader. *Introducing Your Child to Islam, Imaan, and Ihsaan*. King's Lynn, Biddles Books, 2019.

Jayyusi, Salma. "Nature Poetry and the Rise of Ibn Khafaja." *The Legacy of Muslim Spain*, 1994.

Khan, Muhammad Mojlum. *Great Muslims Of The West*. Kube Publishing Ltd, 2017.

Kritzeck, James, editor. *Anthology of Islamic Literature : From the Rise of Islam to Modern Times*. Meridian, 1964.

Nasr, Seyyed. *The Heart of Islam : Enduring Values for Humanity*. New York, Harpercollins, 2002.

Nass, Ihsān al-. *Hassān ibn Thābit, hayātuhu wa-shiʿruhu*. Beirut: Dār al-Fikr al-Hadīth, 1965.

Osman, Khazri, and Faizol Azham Mohamed. "The Aesthetics in the Poems of Patience of Imam Shafi'i Rahimahullah." *International Journal of Academic Research in Business and Social Sciences*, vol. 8, no. 9, 7 Oct. 2018, 10.6007/ijarbss/v8-i9/4868. Accessed 9 Aug. 2021.

Pickthall, Marmaduke. *The Meaning of the Glorious Quran*. Amana Publications, 1996.

Safi, Omid. "Ripening of Love: An Ode to Rumi on the Anniversary of His Death." *The on Being Project*, 17 Dec. 2015, onbeing.org/blog/ripening-of-love-an-ode-to-rumi-on-the-anniversary-of-his-death/?fbclid=IwAR1BxNEtN-_noHU5cjONQhd28ubSdqdbUmok4_a6_5S3RoCTuSsVr5lHPT0. Accessed 20 Dec. 2021.

Sardar, Ziauddin. *What Do Muslims Believe?* Walker & Company, 2007.

Shafi'i, Imam. *Al-Imām Muḥammad Ibn Idris Al-Shāfiʿi's Al-Risāla Fī Uṣūl Al-Fiqh : Treatise on the Foundations of Islamic Jurisprudence*. Translated by Majid Khadduri, Cambridge, Islamic Texts Society, 1997.

Stetkevych, Suzanne, editor. *Early Islamic Poetry and Poetics*. Routledge, 2009.

The National News. "UAE Mars Mission: Who Was the Iraqi Poet Whose Words Inspired Nasa?" *The National*, 9 Feb. 2021, www.thenationalnews.com/uae/science/uae-mars-mission-who-was-the-iraqi-poet-whose-words-inspired-nasa-1.1163246.

Upton, Charles. *Doorkeeper of the Heart: Versions of Rabia*. Threshold Books, 1988.

Vehapi, Flamur. *A Cup with Rumi: Poems*. Al-Albani Publishers, 2015.

___ *The Alchemy of Mind: Poems*. CS Publishing, 2016.

Waqidi, Muhammad ibn ʻUmar al-. *Kitāb al-maghāzī lil-Wāqidī*. Edited by Marsden Jones. 3 vols. University of Oxford Press, 1966.

# Notes

1 Excerpt from "Ripening of Love: An Ode to Rumi on the Anniversary of His Death" by Omid Safi, 2015.

2 Hasan hadith in *Sunan at-Tirmidhi*, 1332.

3 This is known as the 'Tala' al-Badru 'Alaynā' poem or *nasheed* said to have been sung during the time of the Prophet *pbuh* in Madinah. A number of versions and translations of this nasheed exist today. Cf. *In the Gardens of Delight* by Y. Emerick, 169-171, 2021.

4 As qtd. in *In Darfur* by al-Tunisi, translated by Humphrey Davies, 74, 2020.

5 Excerpt from *Doorkeeper* of the Heart by Charles Upton, 52, 1988.

6 Excerpt from "The Aesthetics in the Poems of Patience of Imam Shafi'i Rahimahullah" by K. Osman and F. A. Mohamed, 1879, 2018.

7 Sakhr was one of al-Khansa's brothers.

8 Excerpt from *Classical Arabic Literature*, selected and translated by Geert Jan Van Gelder, 12-14, 2013.

9 Cf. Hadith 34 from the *Forty Hadith of Imam an-Nawawi*.

10   Excerpt from *A Treasury of Virtues* by al-Qudai, 115, 2016. Verses translated by T. Qutbuddin.

11   Poem originally published in *A Cup with Rumi*, 55, 2015. Modified.

12   Excerpt from "The Aesthetics in the Poems of Patience of Imam Shafi'i Rahimahullah" by K. Osman and F. Mohamed, 1878, 2018.

13   Excerpt from *You Were Created to Be a Star Not a Burning Meteor* by Burhan Al-Din Fili, 15, 2012. Modified.

14   Poem originally published in *A Cup with Rumi*, 79, 2015. Modified.

15   Excerpt from *Classical Arabic Literature*, selected and translated by Geert Jan Van Gelder, 66, 2013.

16   Poem originally published in *The Alchemy of Mind*, 25, 2016. Modified.

17   Ibn Thabit about Prophet Muhammad *pbuh*. As qtd. in *Introducing Your Child to Islam, Imaan, and Ihsaan* by Abdul Qader Ismail, 12, 2019.

18   Poem originally published in *The Alchemy of Mind*, 96, 2018. Modified.

19   Ibn Thabit after the passing away of Prophet Muhammad *pbuh*. Excerpt from *Hassan Ibn Thabit, a True Mukhadram*, dissertation by Jennifer Boutz, 40, 2009.

20   Poem originally published in A Cup with Rumi, 93, 2015. Modified.

21   Excerpt from "The Aesthetics in the Poems of Patience of Imam Shafi'i Rahimahullah" by K. Osman and F. A. Mohamed, 1881, 2018.

22   Excerpt from *The Heart of Islam* by Seyyed H. Nasr, 273, 2002.

23   Excerpt from *Al-Ghazali's Letter to a Disciple*, translated by Tobias Mayer, 2005.

24   Excerpt from *The Album of Aphorisms*, translated by Flamur Vehapi, 33, 2019. Modified.

25   *Iqrah*, meaning read, recite or relate, was the first word revealed to the Prophet Muhammad *pbuh* in the Qur'an. See Glossary.

26   Excerpt from *Doorkeeper of the Heart* by Charles Upton, 24, 1988.

27   Emre expresses his yearning to visit the Prophet *pbuh* in Madinah. Excerpt from *Celebrating Muhammad*, collected by Asani and Abdel-Malek, 24, 1995.

28   Inspired by one of the sayings of Ibn-ul Qayyim, a scholar of Islam.

29   Excerpt from *In the Gardens of Delight* by Yahiya Emerick, 326, 2021.

30   Qur'anic inspiration.

31   Excerpt from *Poems from the Straight Path* by Joel Hayward, 6, 2017.

32   Excerpt from *Tulip in the Desert*, translated by Mustansir Mir, 16, 2000.

33   Inspired by a saying of the Prophet Muhammad *pbuh*.

34   Excerpt from *The Album of Aphorisms*, translated by Flamur Vehapi, 26, 2019.

35   Inspired by one of the sayings of Abu Bakr as-Siddiq.

36   Excerpt from *Tulip in the Desert*, translated by Mustansir Mir, 44, 2000.

37   Excerpt from *Anthology of Islamic Literature*, edited by Kritzeck, 239-249, 1964. Verses translated by R. A. Nicholson.

38   Excerpt from *Purification of the Heart*, translated by Hamza Yusuf, 12-13, 2004.

39   As qtd. by S. Haider in "Iqbal and His Philosophy" in Allamaiqbal.com.

40   Greta Thunberg, climate activist from Sweden.

41   As qtd. on The National when NASA congratulated UAE's Hope probe team project, 2021.

42   Excerpt from *The Album of Aphorisms*, translated by Flamur Vehapi, 29, 2019. Modified.

43   Excerpt from *You Were Created to Be a Star Not a Burning Meteor* by Burhan Al-Din Fili, 16, 2012.

44   Excerpt from *Tulip in the Desert*, translated by Mustansir Mir, 18, 2000.

45   Excerpt from *Doorkeeper of the Heart* by Charles Upton, 52, 1988.

46   Excerpt from *The Life of Muhammad* by Ibn Hisham, translated by A. Guillaume, 795, 1955.

47   Excerpt from *Poems from the Straight Path* by Joel Hayward, 16, 2017.

48   Cf. *Diwan of Hassan Ibn Thabit*, edited by Walid N. ʿArafat, 1971; *Hasan Ibn Thabit ibn Thabit al-ansari shahr al-Islam* by Rabiʿa Abu al-Faadil, 1993; *Hassan Ibn Thabit, a True Mukhadram* (dissertation) by Jennifer Boutz, 2009.

49   Cf. *Arab Women Writers*, translated by Mandy McClure, 2008.

50   Cf. *The Book of Great Quotes*, edited by Flamur Vehapi, 2018.

51   Cf. *Arab Women Writers*, translated by Mandy McClure, 2008.

52   Cf. *Al-Imām Muḥammad Ibn Idris Al-Shāfiʿi's Al-Risāla Fī Uṣūl Al-Fiqh: Treatise on the Foundations of Islamic Jurisprudence*, translated by Majid Khadduri, 1997.

53   Cf. *Poems of Al-Mutanabbi*, translated by A. J. Arberry, 1967.

54   Cf. *The Alchemy of Happiness*, translated and edited by C. Field and E. I. Daniel, 1991.

55   Cf. *The Legacy of Muslim Spain*, edited by S. Jayyusi, 381, 1994.

56   Cf. Ciabattari, "Why Is Rumi the Best-Selling Poet in the US?" 2014.

57   Cf. Ali, "The Erasure of Islam from the Poetry of Rumi." The New Yorker, 2017.

58   Cf. *Great Muslims of the West* by Muhammad M. Khan, 2017.

59   Cf. *Purification of the Heart*, translated by Hamza Yusuf, 2004.

60   Cf. *Shikwa & Jawab Shikwa: The Complaint and the Answer*, translated by Abdussalam Puthige, 2020; Tulip in the Desert, translated by Mustansir Mir, 2000.

61   Cf. *You Were Created to Be a Star Not a Burning Meteor* by Burhan Al-Din Fili, 2012.

62   Cf. *A Kaleidoscope of Stories: Muslim Voices in Contemporary Poetry*, edited by R. S. Spiker, 2020.

63   Excerpts from the *Meanings of the Glorious Quran*. Translated by M. Pickthall, 1996.

64   Excerpts from *What do Muslims Believe?* by Sardar, 119-122, 2007, and the primary sources of hadith such as *Sahih Bukhari* and *Sahih Muslim*.

## About the author

**FLAMUR VEHAPI** is a researcher, chronologist, poet, literary translator, academic, and success coach. He received his B.S. in Counseling Psychology with a minor in History from Southern Oregon University, and his M.A. in Conflict Resolution from Portland State University. Currently, he is an Education and Leadership Ph.D. student at Pacific University. In 2009, Flamur received the Imagine Award for Community Peacemaking. He taught social sciences at Rogue Community College and Southern Oregon University, after which he taught at various institutions in the Middle East. He has authored several books and translated two of Sami Frashëri's works. He has worked as a contributing writer for the PSU Chronicles. Flamur and his family currently live in Oregon.

# Other titles by Crescent Books

*The Adhan:* A Brief Chronology by Flamur Vehapi, 2026
*Belief and the Human Mind* by Imad Bayoun, 2026
*Braving Grief* by Tasneem Rahman, 2025
*A Breeze from the East* by Wael Almahdi, 2025
*The Expansion of Islam* by Sami Frashëri, 2025
*The Book of Great Quotes* by Flamur Vehapi, 2025
*Grains of Destiny* by Brandon Mayfield, 2024
*When My Absence Becomes a Moon* by Laureta Rexha, 2024
*Berke Khan of the Golden Horde* by Flamur Vehapi, 2024
*The World According to Sami Frashëri* by Flamur Vehapi, 2024
*The Spectacular Escape* by Burhan Al-Din Fili, 2023
*Atheism Versus Belief* by Brandon Mayfield, 2023
*Kosovo: A Brief Chronology* by Flamur Vehapi, 2023
*Verses of the Heart* by Flamur Vehapi, 2021
*Ertugrul Ghazi: A Very Short Biography* by Flamur Vehapi, 2021

For our titles in other languages, check out thecrescentbooks.com.

## About Crescent Books

Crescent Books is committed to publishing works that challenge the conventional and celebrate the diverse voices that enrich our understanding of faith, culture, and history. As a small, passionate team of book lovers, we guide authors through the publishing process with editorial freedom and genuine partnership. We serve our communities by producing books that inspire, provoke thought, and entertain, creating transformative reading experiences that connect with a broad audience and open doors to new perspectives on our ever-evolving world.

# Personal notes

www.ingramcontent.com/pod-product-compliance
Lightning Source LLC
Chambersburg PA
CBHW030000050426
42451CB00006B/74